WHOAH!

Eight years of bizarre cartoons from
the pages of **Doctor Who Magazine**

Whoah!

This edition first published October 2014 by Miwk Publishing Ltd.
Miwk Publishing, 12 Marbles Way, Tadworth, Surrey KT20 5LW.

ISBN 978-1-908630-73-5

The author and publisher wish to thank **Panini** and **Doctor Who Magazine** for their help in the creation of this book.

A CIP catalogue record for this book is available from the British Library.

Book layout by Robert Hammond.

Printed and bound by CPI Group (UK) Ltd, Croydon, CR0 4YY.

www.miwkpublishing.com
This product was lovingly Miwk made.

FROM THE AUTHOR'S MOUTH

I found **Doctor Who**, oddly enough, when it had been off the air for nearly three years, thanks to an amazing early 90s exhibition at the sadly missed Museum Of The Moving Image in London.

I was too young to have seen it on TV but I fell in love and quickly introduced it to my passion for drawing, and soon there were '**Who** scribbles everywhere.

Soon afterwards, I found our beloved **Doctor Who Magazine** and, staring at the hilarious cartoons on those hallowed pages, I thought to myself,

"I'd like to do that job when I grow up."

So as soon as I grew up I did - and here's the proof!

Big thanks to Tom, Pete and Clay, Matt and Robert, Leighton, me dear old Dad and everyone's best friend, The Doctor.

JAMIE

BOX

FOREWORD IN TIME

"There's no point in being grown up if you can't be childish, sometimes..."

For a TV show that can be remarkably silly, we **Doctor Who** fans can't half take it seriously sometimes. I'm as guilty as anyone. As editor of **Doctor Who Magazine** for the past seven years, I must have published close to seven million words on our daft little show – and quite a few of those words have taken it very seriously indeed. So thank goodness for Jamie Lenman. Jamie's **Doctor Whoah** cartoons have been a much-loved part of **DWM**'s make-up over the last few years, and they've always provided a welcome chuckle as an antidote to our more serious pontifications elsewhere in the magazine.

Doctor Whoah resurrected a proud tradition for **DWM**. The wonderful Tim Quinn and Dicky Howett's irreverent **Doctor Who?** cartoon strip had first appeared on the magazine's letters pages in 1982, running until the mid-1990s. Since then, Leighton Noyes' **Doctor Oho** and Nick Miller's **Nix View** had come and gone, and a few other ideas had been tried and dropped ('comedy' sidebar *Fool Circle* never quite took off), and by 2005 the letters page was definitely missing something...

When Jamie first submitted some ideas to myself and then-**DWM**-editor Clayton Hickman, we were won over straight away. To be a successful cartoonist, you need to be able to come up with a funny gag, and have a unique artistic style, and it was clear that Jamie was blessed with both of these skills. Jamie would always send in a list of potential jokes each month, and we would pick one for him to bring to life, in his own inimitable style. We'd never be quite sure what we were going to get, because until we saw the final artwork, the full impact would be impossible to judge.

Why did Jamie always draw Paul McGann with whiskers, like a cat? Why did he draw Joan Redfern with her hair in the shape of a teapot? Is there a reason why Jon Pertwee is morphing into the Giant Robot?! I still don't know the answer to any of these things – but I do know that **Doctor Whoah** always made me laugh. And that was the whole point.

Tom Spilsbury, Editor **Doctor Who Magazine** 2007 - present

DOCTOR WHOAH!
by baxter
Christmas 2005: A bad phone line between Russell T Davies' flat and the BBC Wales design department means that 50 extras dressed as sticklebacks have to be hastily re-costumed.
EH? SYCO-WHATS?
INVASION SCRIPT
BBC
STICKLEBACKS STRONG!
STICKLEBACKS MIGHTY!
STICKLEBACKS FRESHWATER!

Here we go then - the first **Doctor Whoah!** Although at the time, I didn't know it would be the first, I thought it was just another practice run until I opened the magazine in **Forbidden Planet** and there it was!

This is probably a good place to explain why these cartoons were published under the pseudonym 'Baxter' (after **TMNT**'s Baxter Stockman) instead of my real name. When the strip started in 2006 I was trying to make my way in the world of rock and roll and I didn't want people to see my name on the strips and confuse the silly pictures with the dead-serious music I was making.

Eight years later and with neither career having reached particularly giddy heights, it doesn't seem to matter so much. Ah, the folly of youth!

DOCTOR WHOAH!
by baxter
New Earth: The design department's plans for 'ultra realistic' cat people proved impractical.
JUST HOW ARE YOU CURING THESE PEOPLE?
MEW?
AAAAAAAHH GET ME OUT OF HERE! I CAN'T BREATHE!!!

DOCTOR WHOAH!
by baxter
After their meeting with Queen Victoria the First, the Doctor and Rose travel forwards in time to meet Queen Victoria the Second.
BLINGARIFFIC!
YER, IT'S THE KOH I NOR, THE GREATEST DIAMOND IN THE WORLD. DAVID BOUGHT IT ME.
WILL YOU SIGN MY DOCTOR WHO BOOKS, MISTER ECCLESTON?

DOCTOR WHOAH!

by baxter

Embarrassment for the Cybercontroller as he learns that he's been walking around all day with his brain showing.

DOCTOR WHOAH!
by baxter
After his horriffic experience with The Wire, the Doctor is understandably jumpy when he bumps into Patrick Stewart, Ainsley Harriott and Grant from *EastEnders*.
AAAARGH! SHE'S TAKEN THEIR FACES! AND SHE'S PUT THEIR CLOTHES ON BACK TO FRONT!
NO DOCTOR, LOOK, THEY'RE JUST FACING THE OTHER WAY...
DO YOU KNOW, SOMEONE ONCE TOLD ME MY FACE IS INCREDIBLY DIFFICULT TO DRAW...
REALLY? ME TOO!
YER, ME AN' ALL

DOCTOR WHOAH!
by baxter
Quick-thinking Doctor pulls a cheeky switch on short-sighted Cult of Skaro.
YEAH, TOO RIGHT! DON'T GO NEAR IT, ROSE...
PROTECT THE GENESIS ARK!

I remember we all liked this one because it reminded us of Leighton Noyes' fantastic **Doctor Oho** cartoon, which had been running in the magazine when I'd been buying it as a kid. I owe an awful lot to Leighton in that I've basically stolen his concept and his illustration style, but we've been in touch over the years and he's been the perfect gentleman about it all, very supportive.

I made a mistake on this one and coloured the blobs on the Black Dalek gold, like on the toy I was using for reference. Clayton saved my skin and coloured them black before it went out - talk about attention to detail! I was always amazed by the care that the editorial team devoted to every square inch of that magazine, but I suppose that's what you gotta do if you want such a classy periodical!

Here's a side-on Dalek I drew that didn't make it in. You can always tell how comfy I am drawing things by how accurate they are. If they're all wobbly and weird it's cos I know them well and I can take risks - you can't take risks with that wonderful design! Every angle is sacred!

DOCTOR WHOAH!
by baxter
Trapped on a parallel Earth, the Doctor recharges the last surviving power cell in the TARDIS by giving it ten years of his life...
LOOK! IT'S "DOCTOR WHO– THE EIGHTIES"!
DOCTOR WHO THE EIGHTIES
OH COME ON, ANYTHING'S BETTER THAN THAT! WHAT ABOUT THE FOURTH DOCTOR HANDBOOK OR SOMETHING? I'D RATHER HAVE THE BLOODY COOKBOOK!

DOCTOR WHOAH!
by baxter
Saturday night at the ex-Doctors club....
ON YER BIKE, WITHNAIL. I'M THE NINTH DOCTOR, NOT YOU. GO AND HANG OUT WITH THOSE OTHER "NOT-REALLY-THE-DOCTOR" DOCTORS.
BUT THEY'RE ALL WEIRDOS!
I.. LIKE.. YOUR... BOW-TIE...
HEY.. CAN YOU SMELL SOMETHING?
SNIFF
OI! I SHOULDN'T BE HERE! I DONE A WHOLE STORY! AND I KISSED A LADY, LIKE THEM NEW ONES KEEP DOING!
I WAS THE ONLY ONE WITH A MOUSTACHE, YOU KNOW
NO ENTRY

DOCTOR WHOAH!
by baxter
The Master terrifies a shop full of children as his latest plan fails miserably.
WELL, LET'S SEE...I DON'T THINK FATHER CHRISTMAS HAS ANY NEW CYCLES OF REGENERATIONS IN HIS SACK...BUT HERE'S A NICE PENCIL FOR YOU!
CONFOUND YOU, YOU RED OAF!
I'LL KEEP THE PENCIL THOUGH.
MUMMY! MICHAEL JACKSON PUSHED IN!

by baxter
DOCTOR WHO
POLICE PUBLIC CALL BOX
Despite her claims, there may have been more men in Sarah Jane's life than she is prepared to admit...
WAIT...WAIT DON'T TELL ME...BRIAN?

DOCTOR WHOAH!
by baxter
1993: Proposed 30th Anniversary Special The Dark Dimension is abandoned due to an argument over the size of Tom Baker's part...
COME OFF IT YOU DIRTY LIAR!
WELL, I HEARD IT WAS TWELVE...
THAT'S LONGER THAN SYLV'S ENTIRE BODY!
TEN.
OI!

DOCTOR WHOAH! by baxter
2072: Cosgrove Hall re-create lost episodes of the *Doctor Who* cartoon with specially filmed live-action inserts.
THE LAST ORIGINAL COPY WAS TAPED OVER WITH AN EPISODE OF PRIMEVAL.
BUT LOOK! IT TURNS OUT WE *DO* ALL END UP DRESSING LIKE IN WARRIORS OF THE DEEP!

DOCTOR WHOAH!
by baxter
ITV continues its plans to knock Doctor Who out of the ratings.
BBC
Upper Boat
IT'S BASICALLY JUST LOTS OF BITS OF WOOD NAILED OVER THE DOOR TO THE STUDIO WHERE THEY FILM DOCTOR WHO!
HMM... I LIKE IT. HOW ABOUT, "...WITH CELEBRITIES"?
itv
itv

I love this one. I'm very pleased with the gag and the drawing, and I finally got to say something about the state of British telly.

These two characters aren't based on anyone real, but I've never forgiven one of them for sacking Colin Baker and trying to kill **Doctor Who** on several occasions.

You might notice, as you read on, that the drawings become subtly less and less amateurish, and I'm hoping this will lend the book an autobiographical charm instead of provoking a spate of refund demands.

The fact is that once you've got a regular gig you're drawing all the time and you can't help but get better - plus **DWM** was a very safe space for me to experiment with various techniques and styles as you'll see throughout the book. It's one of many, many things I have to thank them for.

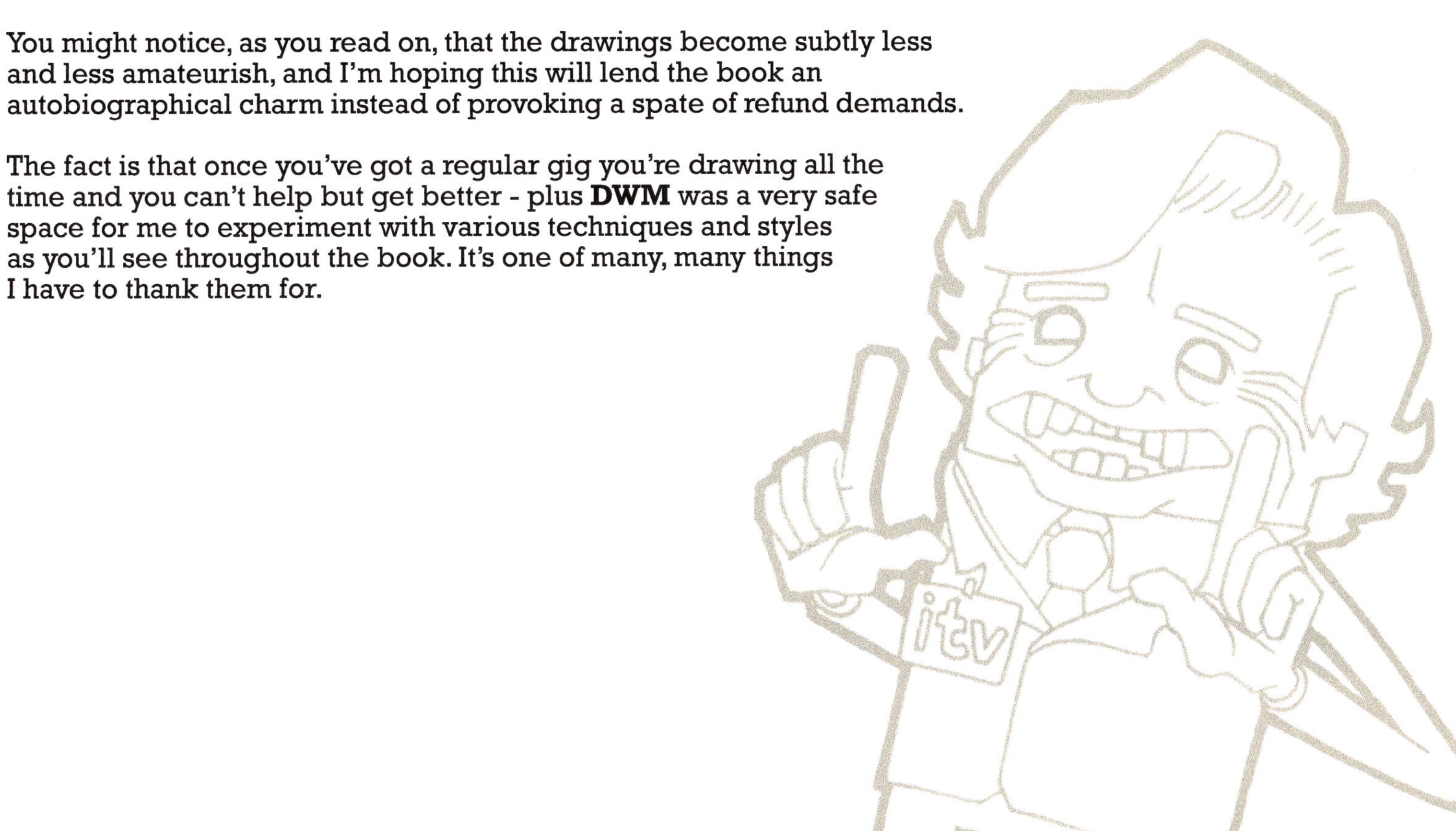

DOCTOR WHOAH!
by baxter
As the Face of Boe finally reveals his important message, the Doctor considers that it might be time to buy an answering machine.
DOCTOR! STEVE CALLED! OH WAIT, WAS IT STEVE? I HAD IT WRITTEN DOWN HERE SOMEWHERE...
...DO YOU HAVE ANY WINDOLENE?

DOCTOR WHOAH!
by baxter
Stike and Varl the sontarans fire their agent after watching *Smith and Jones.*
THEY WANTED A CHUNKY, MILITARISTIC ALIEN RACE! LOOK AT US! YOU SHOULD HAVE BEEN STRAIGHT ONTO THAT ONE! YOU HAVEN'T GOT US ANY WORK SINCE JIM'LL BLOODY FIX IT!
OH, SO WHO WAS IT THAT GOT YOU THAT WEEK ON EASTENDERS, DOUBLING FOR THE MITCHELL BROTHERS?

John Smith shows Joan some of the weird monsters and familiar faces in his book.

'THE DOCTOR WHO YEARBOOK 1995'?

YES, I DREAMT WE WERE ALL RUNNING ROUND A PLACE CALLED "ALBERT SQUARE", AND IT WAS ALL A BIT POINTLESS...

WHO WAS THAT TERRIBLE WOMAN?

DOC–I MEAN HUGH GRA– I MEAN JOHN SMITH LOOK OUT! ALL OF THE VILLAGE'S BIZARRELY IDENTICAL AND CONVENIENTLY SCOWLING SCARECROWS ARE COMING ALIVE!!!

RATTATTA

DOCTOR WHOAH!
The Doctor reminds the Master of their times together in a bid to pull him through his injury.
REMEMBER ON TRAKEN, WHEN YOU PAINTED YOUR TEETH ONTO YOUR LIPS? AND THAT TIME WHEN YOU DRESSED UP LIKE A SCARE-CROW AND STOOD IN A FIELD ALL DAY FOR NO REASON AT ALL?
AH YES...I WAS AN IDIOT THEN...

DOCTOR WHOAH!
Some of the 'Classic' Doctors feel understandably aggrieved by the exciting regenerations experienced by the Ninth Doctor and the Master.
HOW COME YOU TWO GET ALL FIREWORKS AND ALL I GOT WAS A SWIRLY BLUE FACE?
YEAH! AND ALL I GOT TO DO WAS THIS STUPID THING WITH MY MOUTH!
YAKKETY YAK YAK
BLAH BLAH
KNICKERS!
KONK
YAK YAK
COUNT YOURSELVES LUCKY, LADS! THIS POOR FELLER DIDN'T GET A REGENERATION AT ALL!
ADRIC?!
OW! YES I DID! HAVEN'T YOU SEEN THEM ALL ON YOUTUBE?

When I was drawing this one a chum asked me what it was all about and I said,

"Well, when the Doctor gets fatally injured or falls over in the TARDIS he changes his whole body and in the past it used to look a bit cheap, whereas in the new show it tends to look spectacular so here's all the old Doctors, mid-change, complaining to the new fellers that they've got better special effects."

He looked at me and said,

"This is the best thing that's ever happened to you, isn't it?"

Pretty much!

Of course then Saint Moffat went and gave us and Sir Paul the big scene we'd all been waiting for, and it was one of the good explode-y ones too, so it's all alright now. ADRIC!?!

DOCTOR WHOAH!
by baxter
An awkward moment as Dalek Caan and one of his pig-slaves bump into Dave the Roboman in Tesco...
OH, HI CAAN. I SEE YOU DON'T WASTE ANY TIME.
WHO'S THIS, CAAN? YOU TOLD ME I WAS THE ONLY AUGMENTED HUMAN SLAVE IN YOUR LIFE!
LOOK...I WAS A DIFFERENT PERSON BACK THEN...

DOCTOR WHOAH!
by baxter
October 2007: Trouble on the door at rehearsals for Children In Need's Fifth Doctor-Tenth Doctor meet-up...
BRAVE HEART, TEGAN!
THERE SHOULD HAVE BEEN ANOTHER WAY!
ER...CRICKET'S BRILLIANT...?
HOLD ON A MINUTE...
BBC CHILDREN INDEED
BBC
Upper Boat

by baxter
DOCTOR WHOAH!
Encouraged by the recent return of the Macra, several 'Classic' monsters eagerly await *'The call'*...
ARE YOU SURE IT'S PLUGGED IN?
GOTTLE OF GEER!

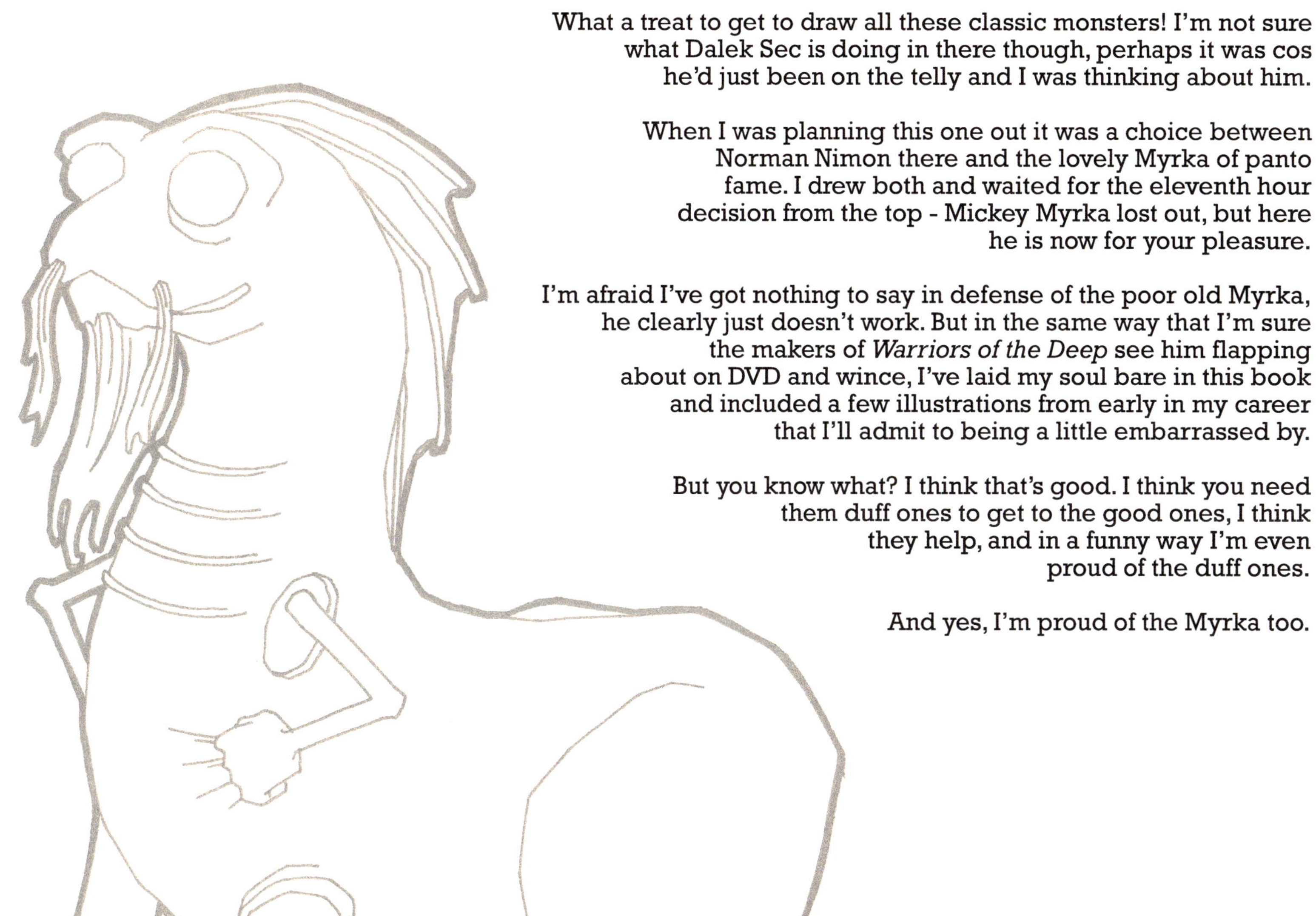

What a treat to get to draw all these classic monsters! I'm not sure what Dalek Sec is doing in there though, perhaps it was cos he'd just been on the telly and I was thinking about him.

When I was planning this one out it was a choice between Norman Nimon there and the lovely Myrka of panto fame. I drew both and waited for the eleventh hour decision from the top - Mickey Myrka lost out, but here he is now for your pleasure.

I'm afraid I've got nothing to say in defense of the poor old Myrka, he clearly just doesn't work. But in the same way that I'm sure the makers of *Warriors of the Deep* see him flapping about on DVD and wince, I've laid my soul bare in this book and included a few illustrations from early in my career that I'll admit to being a little embarrassed by.

But you know what? I think that's good. I think you need them duff ones to get to the good ones, I think they help, and in a funny way I'm even proud of the duff ones.

And yes, I'm proud of the Myrka too.

DOCTOR WHOAH! by baxter
Christmas on board the *Valiant*.
WOW LOOK I GOT A LAUGHING RING! THESE CRACKERS ARE BRILLIANT!
HA HA HA
TEE HEE HEE!
I'M DEFINITELY HAVING THAT...
MENTAL
REAL OLD
CAT
DOGTOR

If this book and my drawing skills were the film **2001: A Space Oddysey**, then drawing in colour would be when the apes saw that first obelisk, and this would be when that other one turned up on the moon. It would also be a much, much better book.

After a few years of scrabbling around in Photoshop and not being particularly happy with the results, I finally found the 'multiply' setting in the layers pallette, which meant I could retain the slightly finer pencil drawings and colour through them, as it were.

I've always liked to keep the drawings scratchy and scruffy, I don't rub any lines out cos even the wrong lines end up adding something to the finished picture. I like to see where things have come from, how you got there.

Anyway this technique allowed me to keep all that stuff and this daring new style debuted in a cracking Christmas strip, full to bursting with little sight-gags, a lovely one this' un.

DOCTOR WHOAH! by baxter
The Heavenly Host get flustered by the big celebrities.
ARE HEAT HERE?
KYLIE MINOGUE ON BOARD, AND US IN OUR NIGHTIES! WE'LL NEVER LIVE IT DOWN!

DOCTOR WHOAH!
by baxter
Jilted Katy Manning tells all about love-rat Dalek.
TYPICAL! GETS HIMSELF A MAKEOVER AND SWANS OFF WITH A YOUNGER MODEL!

DOCTOR WHOAH!
by baxter
Sally Sparrow tries to make sense of the Doctor's cryptic wallpaper message...
BEWARE
THE WEEPING ANGEL
OH, AND DUCK!
...AND DUCK?
BOO HOO! LET'S GET HER!
YEAH! SOB...

DOCTOR WHOAH! by baxter
More notable *Doctor Who* deaths. #101: In a display of his manipulative powers, the Seventh Doctor literally *confuses* the Black Dalek to death...
YOU ARE DEFEATED, DALEK. YOUR HOME PLANET IS DESTROYED, YOUR LEADER, DAVROS, IS DEAD. WELL, ACTUALLY IT'S A BIT HARD TO TELL, ISN'T IT? COS HE MIGHT ACTUALLY GO ON TO BECOME THE EMPEROR DALEK WE SAW IN *'EVIL OF THE DALEKS'*, WHICH IS TECHNICALLY IN THE PAST... OR IT MIGHT EVEN BE ANOTHER INFLATABLE DUMMY LIKE ON NECROS ...HERE, WHY DON'T YOU READ *'WAR OF THE DALEKS'* BY JOHN PEEL? I'M SURE IT'LL MAKE IT ALL CLEAR...
ARGH! SUCH CONVOLUTED PLOTLINES!

DOCTOR WHOAH!
by baxter
The Doctor gets in a bit of trouble on the Planet of Hats.
INFIDEL! HIS HEAD IS BARE!
DESTROY THE HAT-LESS ONE!
I FLIPPIN' TOLD YOU...

I decided at this point that the 'coloured oval' I'd previously relied upon didn't really do justice to the desolate wastelands of the Planet Of Hats, so I started drawing simple vector backgrounds that would hopefully compliment the main illo but also help it to stand out.

This seemed like a very clever idea when all I had to draw was a moonscape and some clouds - seemed less clever when it came to things like the Eleventh Doctor's TARDIS interior. This planet background became my very own gravel quarry - you'll be seeing it again a fair few times, and in fact you can see it on the back cover!

I can't take credit for the Planet Of Hats though, that's a Tom Spilsbury original. We'll be seeing that again too!

DOCTOR WHOAH!
by baxter
After the two UNIT episodes, some fans are left disappointed by the absence of a particular character...
WHERE WAS HE?!
WHERE WAS MIKE YATES!?
I ♥ MIKE YATES
YEAH! DID YOU SEE HIM IN "DIMENSIONS IN TIME?
THE CHARACTER WAS VAGUELY RECOGNISABLE!!
POP!
OPERATION
HOLD ON LADS!
I'VE JUST READ ON THIS FORUM THAT HE IS COMING BACK, IN THE LAST EPISODE... HAVING TRAVELLED BACK-WARDS IN TIME ON A PARALLEL EARTH TO MARRY ADRIC AND BECOME OMEGA!!!
MIKE WAS RIGHT
TWODDLE.COM
ME TOO

DOCTOR WHOAH!
by baxter
What the Hath were *really* saying...
BUBBLE BLURP BOP BIPPLE PIP!
Hey, guess what! This war's only been going on for seven days!
BLOORP BOOP BUP BUPPLE POP BURP.
Yeah! And whatever you do, don't go outside, you'll probably die.
>SIGH<...IF ONLY WE COULD COMMUNICATE SOMEHOW...COME ON, LET'S GET TO THE SURFACE! IT'S THE ONLY WAY TO SOLVE THIS MYSTERY!
BLURPLE BOP
Oh, bloody hell
SUPER SOAKER
SUPER SOAKER

DOCTOR WHOAH! by baxter
Sarah Jane holds it together for Luke's benefit.
EXTERMINATE! EXTERMINATE! EXTERMINATE!
MISTER SMIFF
STILL GOT IT
OH GOD, YOU'RE SO YOUNG! THEY'RE GOING TO KILL YOU! THEY'RE GOING TO FRY YOUR BONES! THEY'RE GOING TO CHOP YOU UP INTO HANDY BITE-SIZE PIECES! BOO HOO HOO!

DOCTOR WHOAH! by baxter
After all they've been through, all they've seen, there's only one thing the Doctor has to say to Davros...
FLOSSING. I REALLY CAN'T STRESS HOW IMPORTANT IT IS. AND YOU MIGHT WANT TO THINK ABOUT BOOKING AN APPOINTMENT WITH THE HYGIENIST - HOW'S TUESDAY FOR YOU?
MIRROR OF RASSILON
DAVR 05

DOCTOR WHOA!
by baxter
The *real* reason *Doctor Who* is banned at the RSC...
...ISSUE #399... NEARLY DONE...
THANK YOU DAVID...
ALAS, P-POOR SOBEK...
DO YOU WANT **MY** AUTOGRAPH? I WAS IN **EXTRAS**, YOU KNOW!
MASSIVE GENIUS
MAGAZINE
ISSUES 259 -400

DOCTOR WHOAH!
by baxter
Ood stylings.
YEAH, MOST OF THE GUYS ROUND HERE GO FOR THE WHOLE "BALD-HEAD-AND-BEARD" COMBO, BUT I JUST LIKE TO LET IT GROW NATURAL!
HE IS AWAKE AND YOU WILL WORSHIP HIM.
!

DOCTOR WHOAH! by baxter
The Brigadier's heroics with the Destroyer have had an unfortunate rub-off effect on his homelife.
GET OFF MY SOFA.
ALISTAIR!

When I drew this, an illustrator chum paid me a huge compliment and said that although it looks nothing like the Brigadier, it also looks exactly like the Brigadier, which is sort of what I'm aiming for I suppose!

I love the Brig, I love **Battlefield**, and I love this gag. Although I think the one about the dog being called Benton is probably even better! I did keep trying to work out a gag where Benton accidentally calls the Brigadier 'Dad' and everyone gets very embarrassed, but I couldn't get it off the ground.

He did always look like it was on the tip of his tongue though, didn't he?

DOCTOR WHOAH!
by baxter
Alone in the TARDIS, the Doctor realises he still has plenty of friends...
HANG ON, THIS AWARD'S FOR JEREMY CLARKSON!

DOCTOR WHOAH!
by baxter
The Mind Robber, 1968: Originally, a much uglier actor was cast to fill in for Frazer Hines as the Doctor fails the 'face fit' task miserably...
OH MY GIDDY AUNT!
HOOTS MON! HOO WULL AH PLAY THE BAGPIPES NOO!?

DOCTOR WHOAH! by baxter
In an earlier version of the Christmas Special, Jackson Lake picks up an entirely different info-stamp and is not convinced he's the Doctor at all…
HOLD ON- WHO ARE YOU?
QUIT YO' JIBBA-JABBA! AH PITY THE FOO' DON'T RECKONNISE MR.T WHEN HE SEES HIM!
ARF?

DOCTOR WHOAH!
by baxter
Dalek-only pilot *The Destroyers* is abandoned when Terry Nation denies himself the rights to use his own Daleks.
THAT'S MY GRANNY! SHE'S VISITING THE STUDIO FOR THE DAY!
AND YOU'RE NOT HAVING DAVROS, NEITHER! COME ON, YOU!
DIRECTOR

DOCTOR WHOAH!
by baxter
Verity Lambert came up with the idea of casting William Hartnell as the First Doctor when she saw him whilst watching dreary 60's kitchen-sink drama *This Sporting Life*.
OH HELLO BILL! DO YOU LIKE THE FILM SO FAR?
WHAT WAS THAT, MY CHILD? OH GOODNESS ME, NO NO NO! I LANDED HERE QUITE MY BISTAKE.

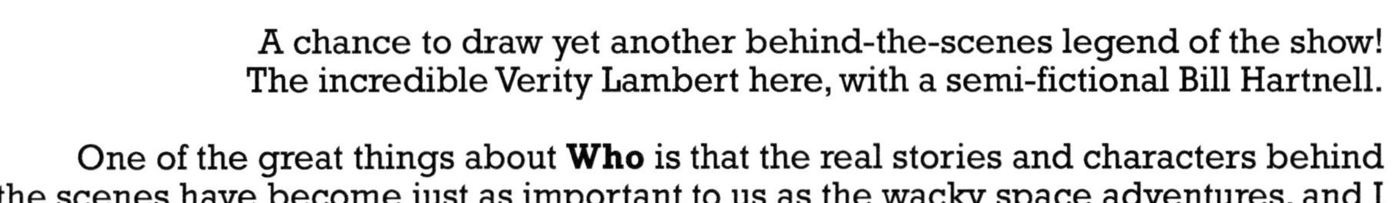

A chance to draw yet another behind-the-scenes legend of the show! The incredible Verity Lambert here, with a semi-fictional Bill Hartnell.

One of the great things about **Who** is that the real stories and characters behind the scenes have become just as important to us as the wacky space adventures, and I think this one celebrates that point. I thought the film they made about these two and all those other pioneers was lovely, very moving.

This Sporting Life is pretty good too! It's got young Dumbledore and the policeman out of *Ghost Light* in it to boot!

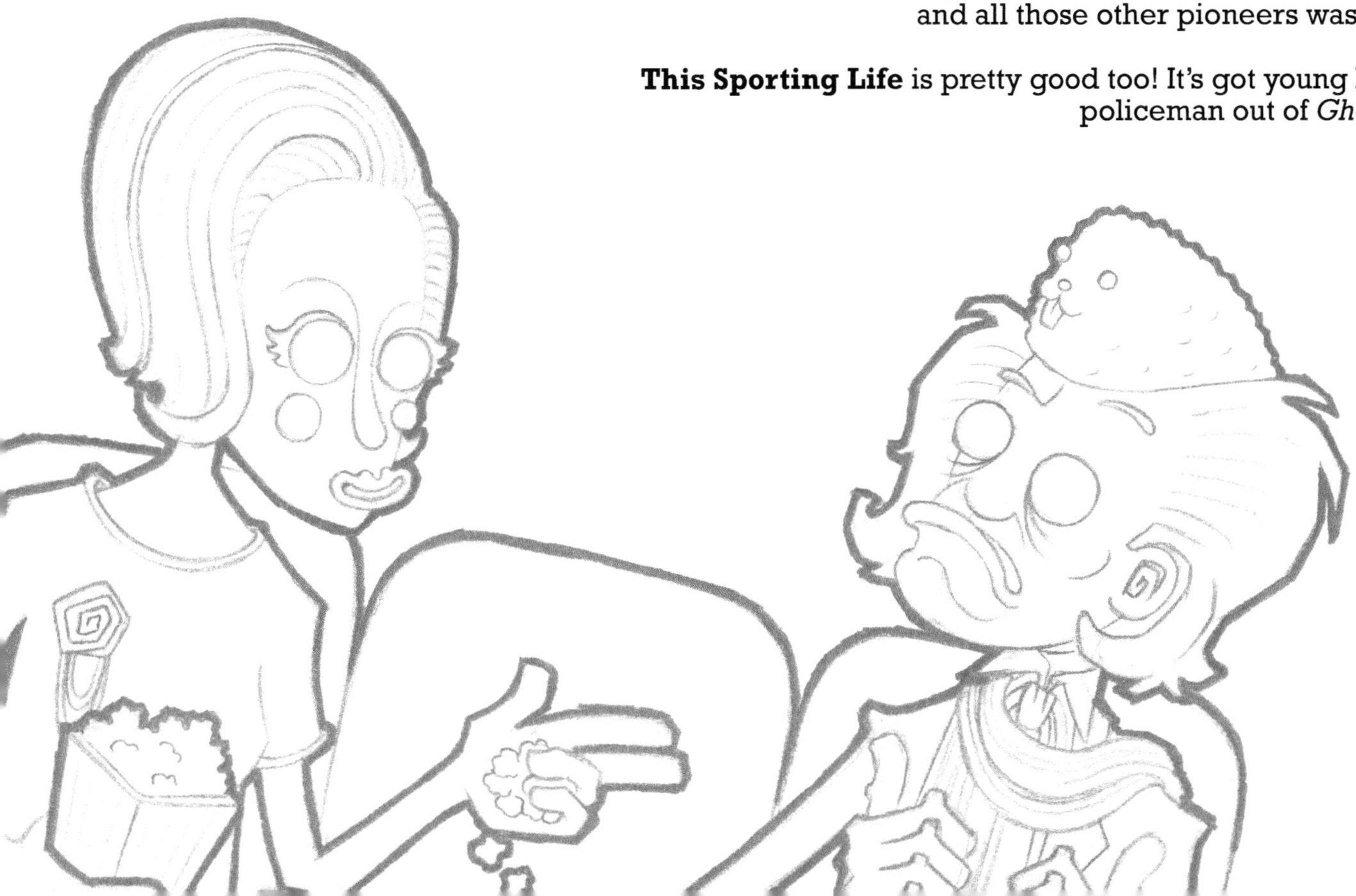

DOCTOR WHOAH!
by baxter
Silver Nemesis was originally called *Yellow Nemesis*...
YOU SEE ACE, AEONS AGO THE TIMELORDS CAME UP WITH THE ULTIMATE DEFENCE FOR GALLIFREY – A LIVING CHEESE!
TAP
TAP

DOCTOR WHOAH!
by baxter
A nasty shock lurks under Omega's helmet...
NO OMEGA, DON'T!
OMEGA, AFTER ALL THESE YEARS ALONE IN YOUR ANTI-MATTER DOMAIN...
I'M AFRAID YOUR HAIR HAS GROWN INTO-
A MULLET! NOOOOO!!!

DOCTOR WHOAH!
by baxter
Tom Baker famously was cast as the Fourth Doctor *just after* he had written a very polite letter to the BBC, asking for an acting job.
THE NEXT DAY...
MRS THE QUEEN
BIG CASTLE
INGLAND
DEAR MR CADBURY
PRETTY PLEASE WILL YOU MAKE ME AN ENTIRE CASTLE OUT OF CHOCO

DOCTOR WHOAH!
by baxter
A familiar aspect of the Fifth Doctor's adventures were the firey arguments with stubborn air-hostess Tegan Jovanka...
JUST BECAUSE I'M AUSTRALIAN, EVERYONE ASSUMES I'M A HUGE MEL GIBSON FAN! THE MAN HASN'T MADE A SINGLE DECENT FILM IN HIS ENTIRE CAREER!
BRAVEHEART, TEGAN!

DOCTOR WHOAH!
by baxter
After his regeneration at the start of *Robot*, the fourth Doctor teases the Brigadier by trying on various ridiculous items of clothing that the Doctor would never sanely wear.
HOW ABOUT THIS THEN?
ZOOP! WHY, I OUGHTTA...!
RAZZA FAZZA WAZZA...

DOCTOR WHOAH!
by baxter
Romantic Eighth Doctor snogs the life out of Grace after she gives him a pair of shoes.
HOW 'BOUT THESE, YOU LIKE THESE? FEELING GOOD ABOUT THIS PAIR?
AH...LOOK, GRACE, IT WAS REALLY A SPUR-OF-THE-MOMENT KIND OF THING...

DOCTOR WHOAH! by baxter
The Seventh Doctor had a cheeky habit of handing over ancient Gallifreyan weapons to his enemies...
ASE
TARGET
I'M SORRY ACE, I REALLY REALLY HONESTLY HAVE LOST THIS TIME. ICE WARRIORS, YOU HAVE DEFEATED ME. TAKE *THE SPHERE OF B'ACKPHIRE* AND GO.
ERM...ACTUALLY, WE'VE DECIDED WE DON'T WANT IT AFTER ALL. I'VE JUST REMEMBERED, WE'VE ALREADY GOT ONE.
ERR...YES! IT'S VERY NICE!

Beware of odd little men bearing gifts!

I was six when *Survival* broadcast, so any memories I do have of catching **Doctor Who** on screen were of Sophie and Sylvester, and it's no surprise they're my favourtie team. I remember how much the tumbling metal letters at the end of the title sequence scared me, and my idea of **Doctor Who** in the background of UK culture was as a strange little fellow, quietly powerful.

I love drawing Ace as the big lug, like Alice the Goon from *Private Olive Oyl*. That's basically their dynamic, right? She's his muscle! It was great to pit these two against the Ice Warriors, seeing as that's where they were headed had the show gone on, and I even managed to squeeze a *Monty Python* reference in there, which is a good day's work for me. Keep your eyes peeled for more of those!

DOCTOR WHOAH!
by baxter
The Ninth Doctor and Rose visit Skrodulon Five, one of the only planets in the universe which does *not* have a north.
EH UP, OUR KID!
YOU WOT GUV? OOZ KID?
WOSSIE ONNERBAHT?

DOCTOR WHOAH!
by baxter
As the Doctor's tenth regeneration looms, bets are being taken as to what will finally finish him off…shot by gangsters? Falling over? Romance?
OH NO, DOCTOR!
WHAT'S HAPPENED TO HIM?
IT LOOKS LIKE...
...HIS FACE HAS BEEN LITERALLY WORN AWAY BY SO MANY KISSES!
HOW HORRIBLE!
DO YOU THINK...
MAYBE... ANOTHER KISS WOULD HELP?
YES, YES! A KISS! A KISS! A KISS!

DOCTOR WHOAH!
by baxter
Eleventh Doctor Matt Smith - cast, among other reasons for his incredibly "Doctor-Who-ish" hair.
PLEASE BOX
I STILL DON'T KNOW WHAT THEY WERE ON ABOUT

DOCTOR WHOAH! by baxter
The universe sings the Doctor to sleep.
♫ SEX BOMB, SEX BOMB... YOU'RE MY SEX BOMB... ♪
ERG! ARE YOU SURE YOU DON'T KNOW ANY PET SHOP BOYS?
BUMP
GRIND
WIB DE BOM
WHAM
DANGE
FALLIN
MASONRY

DOCTOR WHOAH!
by baxter
Sutekh is furious as the Doctor travels to his tomb in Cairo and breaks his concentration.
YOU INTERFERING INSECT! I WAS ABOUT TO BEAT THE HIGH SCORE!
GAME OVER

DOCTOR WHOAH!
by baxter
The Doctor scares the Atraxi away from Earth with a deafening, high-pitched noise.
ARGH! WHAT IS THAT PAINFUL FREQUENCY?
SQUEEEEEEEEEEEEEE
IT'S THE SOUND OF THOUSANDS OF DOCTOR WHO FANS ACROSS THE UK "SQUEE"-ING AT THAT PICTURE OF A SEA DEVIL. YOU'D BETTER CLEAR OFF BEFORE I ROLL OUT THE ZYGONS.

DOCTOR WHOAH! by baxter
Having the Earth suddenly explode into a swirling void can be good for avoiding tricky questions.
HAVE YOU SEEN THAT TENNER I LEFT ON THE COFFEE TABLE?
ERM... OH WOW LOOK!

It's hard to be topical with a monthly magazine, and it's even harder when the interweb knows everything before you do. Quite often the editors and I were trying to come up with gags about episodes we hadn't even seen!

Just an episode title, a few press shots, make that funny if you can.

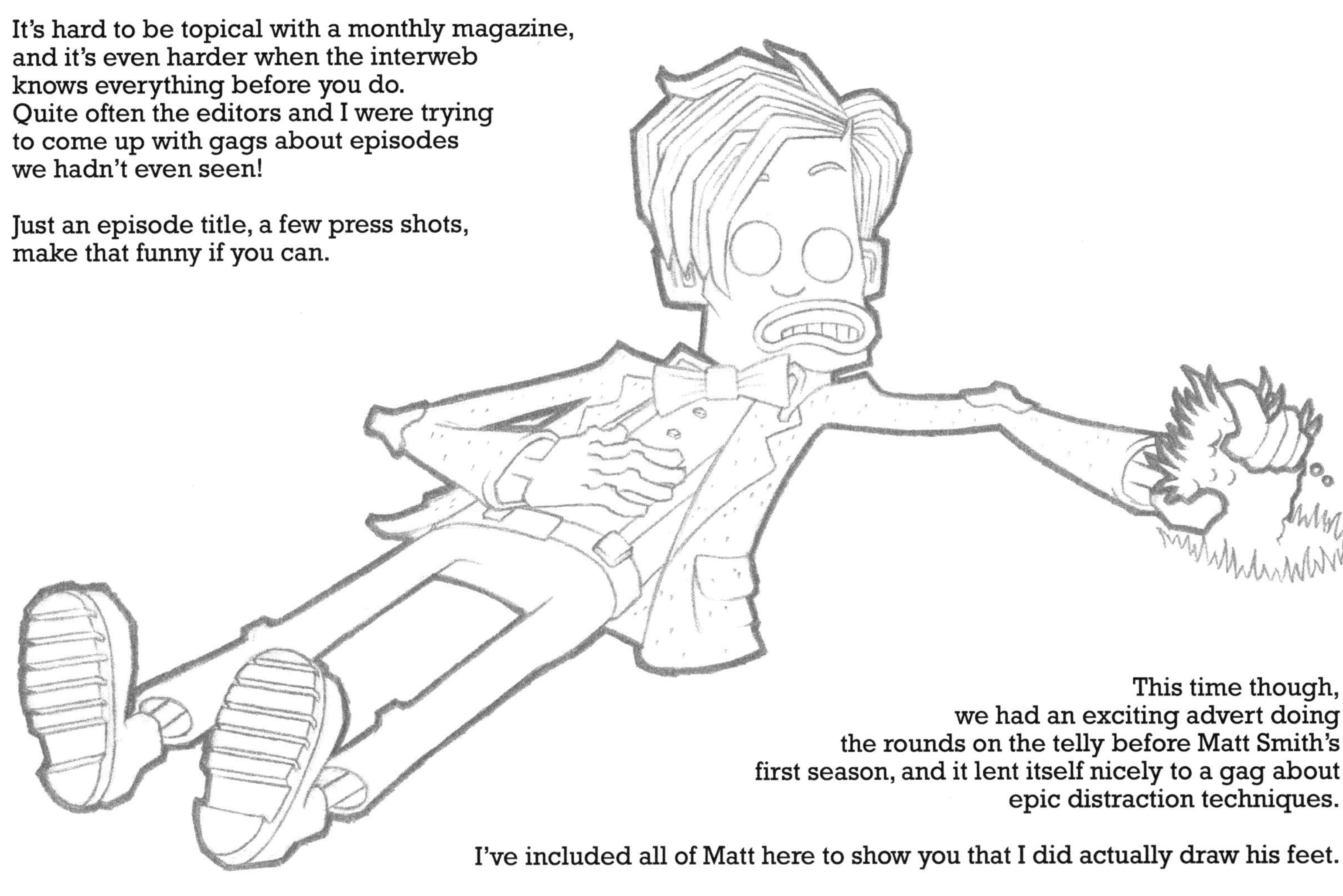

This time though, we had an exciting advert doing the rounds on the telly before Matt Smith's first season, and it lent itself nicely to a gag about epic distraction techniques.

I've included all of Matt here to show you that I did actually draw his feet.

DOCTOR WHOAH! by baxter
Biting Amy's stone hand turns out to be a mistake.
ALRIGHT, I BELIEVE YOU. NOW WE REALLY ARE GOING TO DIE.
BBC one
Coming up next:
Someone Gets Fired
tee hee! ho ho!

DOCTOR WHOAH!
by baxter
The Silurian name debate is finally put to rest.
THEY'RE CALLED SILURIANS. OR AS SOME PEOPLE WOULD ARGUE, THE "EOCENES"...
ACTUALLY, WE'RE CALLED THE "BUFFINS", AND OUR AQUATIC COUSINS THE "RIMPLE-TIMPLES" AREN'T TOO PLEASED WITH THE NICK-NAME YOU GAVE THEM, EITHER.

DOCTOR WHOAH! by baxter
Blundering Ogrons miss the Stonehenge meet-up by a few hundred miles.
IS OGRON SURE THIS IS RIGHT ANCIENT MONUMENT?
YES. TRUST OGRON! OTHER ALIENS JUST FASHIONABLY LATE.
HADRIAN'S WALL

Ogrons! So much comic potential and yet they only appeared in the strip once.

I loved going a bit off piste with the strip - I know everyone loves Daleks and Cybermen but sometimes you just want to draw Hadrian's Wall and a load of sheep. And look at that scenery!

I should have drawn the Ogron ship as a Fairy Liquid bottle though.
You can tell I was nervous about it.

DOCTOR WHOAH!
by baxter
River Song is brought to trial on the Planet of Hats...
DOCTOR RIVER SONG!
YOU STAND ACCUSED OF MURDERING AN INNOCENT FEZ!!!
INFIDEL! HER HEAD IS BARE!!!
JUSTICE FOR FEZ

DOCTOR WHOAH!
PWEEEEEEP
by baxter
The original Cybermen were a human-like race who had gradually replaced all their body parts.
ERM...I'M NOT SURE YOU'VE GOT THE RIGHT IDEA...
FRIGIDA

DOCTOR WHOAH!
by baxter
Jo Grant confesses to Sarah Jane that her 1970s marriage didn't last...
YES, IT'S SAD. BUT AT LEAST I'VE STILL GOT THE KIDS!
AUN-TIE SA-RAH!
DESTRO... ER... AUN-TIE SA-RAH!

DOCTOR WHOAH!
by baxter
The TARDIS crew open their Christmas presents...
OH! ANOTHER TIE... THANK YOU, AMY... AGAIN...
docter x x
wear this tonight x love A x x
DAPOL
SUPER REALISTIC "DOCTOR" MASK

DOCTOR WHOAH! by baxter

You can keep your Ernie Wise - as far as I'm concerned the greatest straight man in British comedy was Nicholas Courtney. How he stood up to all the Doctor's antics without even wobbling his lip is beyond me. He even manages to command your respect in his skimpies!

This one and the Axos one in a couple of strips' time are two of my absolute faves in the whole set...I love the double act between the Third Doctor and the Brig, I love how flustered he is here.

And I'm especially proud because I managed to sneak in a gag from the great **Doctor Oho**, whose kinky spying Daleks were always muttering about cream sprinkles or some such saucy delicacy.

Choccy-licky!

DOCTOR WHOAH!
by baxter
The Doctor cruelly ignores dying Abigail's Christmas wish...
WHERE DO YOU WANT TO GO, ABIGAIL? ANYWHERE IN SPACE AND TIME!
ERG... A HOSPITAL?
YAAAAAAAY, THE PYRAMIDS! WHOOP!

DOCTOR WHOAH! by baxter
The Axons offer Earth a miracle substance that can replicate anything else on the planet.
PLAY-DOH!
DOH
LOOK! I'VE MADE A HAMBURGER!
WHO

DOCTOR WHOAH! by baxter

The loss of Nick Courtney in 2011 was one of several crushing blows we've suffered over the last few years, and I was incredibly proud and grateful for the space in the magazine with which to pay my public and personal respects to the lovely man.

I understand that the readers appreciated the sentiment, which makes me doubly proud. Seen below here is a sketch sent for discussion with the editorial team.

by baxter
Look behind you...
WHAT WAS THAT?
WHY DID YOU SCREAM JUST THEN?
I'VE NO IDEA! AND WHERE'S MY SANDWICH GONE?

DOCTOR WHOAH!
by baxter
Idris is furious when a girl with the soul of Bessie turns up.
OH AND WHO'S THIS? YOUR BIT ON THE SIDE?
LOOK, IT WAS A LONG TIME AGO! SHE HELPED ME THROUGH A VERY DIFFICULT PERIOD... I HAD A STRESSFUL NEW JOB, YOU WERE BEING TOTALLY UNRESPONSIVE...
BEEP BEEP!
PLEASE

DOCTOR WHOAH!
by baxter
Colonel Manton realises he's sent his request for help to the wrong monastery.
SO - LET ME GET THIS STRAIGHT ... YOU'RE THE ARMLESS MONKS? DOES THAT MEAN NO ELECTRIC SWORDS?
I'M AFRAID SO, YES. TERRIBLY SORRY. BUT WE ARE FEROCIOUS KICKERS!
THREATENING WAGGLE

TORCHWHOAH! by baxter

Jack and Gwen investigate...

NOPE, THE FLAME-THROWER DIDN'T DO IT EITHER. OK, BRING IN THE POISONOUS ANTS AND THE RASPBERRY JAM!

CAN'T SOMEONE ELSE HAVE A TURN?

DOCTOR WHOAH! by baxter

DOCTOR WHOAH!
by baxter
The search for baby Melody continues...
...WE'VE ENLISTED TWO MORE OF OUR SASSY, DANGEROUS FRIENDS TO HELP FIND BABY MELODY...
...DOCTOR, MEET SYMPHONY STREAM AND HARMONY LAKE!
HELLO...
...SWEETIE?

DOCTOR WHOAH!
by baxter
Craig's new lodger is even odder than the last one.
NOW, ER... SIMON... I DON'T KNOW WHEN THIS LITTLE GUY ARRIVED, BUT THE TENANCY AGREEMENT DEFINITELY SAYS "NO PETS"...
SILENCE. YOU ARE INTERRUPTING DESPERATE HOUSEWIVES.
MONDAS
KRISPZ
Castrol

I had a great time with this one, I went overboard with the sight gags on the Cyberman there, tried to go as silly as possible and still keep him recogniseable.

My philosophy for this sort of thing and basically my whole approach to the style of the characters was that I wanted it to look like it had been drawn by someone who's seen **Doctor Who**, but only vaguely remembered it.

So Cybermen, they had the big ears with the straws in and the tube sign on their chests, right? Jon Pertwee - was he the one who had his hair in the shape of a giant shell? Who was the one who was a lion?

You get the idea. Or maybe you don't!

DOCTOR
H!
by baxter
Everyone must wear an 'eye drive' in order to remember the Silents.
HOW COME YOU'RE WEARING TWO?
INCREDIBLY FORGETFUL, SAH!

by baxter
Christmas,1972.
OH DOCTOR, DO YOU LIKE IT? I KNITTED IT ESPECIALLY FOR YOU! DIG THAT CRAZY PATTERN!
MY DEAR JO, WHY, IT'S DELIGHTFUL! I PROMISE I SHALL WEAR IT EVERY DAY...
...WHEN I GO COMPLETELY INSANE...

DOCTOR WHOAH!
by baxter
Frazer Hines talks fondly about the missing episodes of *The Underwater Menace.*
...AND THEN, AFTER I'D COMPLETED THE TRIPLE SOMERSAULT OFF THE TOP OF THE SET INTO THE PADDLING POOL, THE GIANT FIRE-BREATHING MECHANICAL FISH CAME IN AND STARTED THE EPIC ROCK-FALL SEQUENCE...
IT'S A SHAME WE'VE LOST THOSE EPISODES NOW...
...ALL YOU CAN HEAR ON THE SOUNDTRACK IS A LOT OF SHUFFLING FEET...
NUSSING IN ZE VURLD KEN SCHTOP ME NAAAVUUUGHHH!!!
TOTAL DUDE

Doctor Whoah goes widescreen! I had no idea at the time why I'd been afforded this special privilege but boy did I make use of it!

All I knew was that I'd been asked to write a strip about *The Underwater Menace*, and there I go and do one that hinges on the episodes being lost, when of course it was all for celebrating their recovery!

I was strongly advised to buy a ticket to a mystery screening at the BFI in London, and there we were all reunited with a true classic, a joy to behold.

I like to think this is one of *my* classics!

DOCTOR WHOAH!
by baxter
Suddenly Amy has a lot of explaining to do.
SONTAR
DOCTOR WHO
I'M NOT *SURE* THAT'S A WATER PISTOL...

DOCTOR WHOAH!
by baxter
Ace's habit of getting his name wrong was starting to get on the Doctor's nerves...
OI PROFESSOR! WATCHA DOOIN'?
THINGS TO DO:
1. Take Ace to haunted house
2. Force Ace to confront horrible Mum
3. Turn Ace into cat-person

DOCTOR WHOAH!
by baxter
PEAS WHAT NOW? BOZ
OFFICIAL TARDIS PLAY-TENT
As the Doctor and Clara begin their travels, he is reminded of something he'd forgotten to do...
WELL, WHAT'S OUT THERE, DOCTOR?
OH, ERR... NOTHING! UMM... LET'S TRY SOMEWHERE ELSE!

DOCTOR WHOAH!
by baxter
The Doctor battles EVERY TYPE OF DALEK EVER...!
HMMM...THE BLUE PETER DALEK CAKE AND THE 60s BUBBLE-BATH DALEK ... NOT EXACTLY TERRIFYING, ARE YOU?
I WILL MAKE YOU FEEL A BIT SICK
AND THEN A SOOTHING BATH!

DOCTOR WHOAH! by baxter

I went through a bit of a crisis at this point and decided the characters I was drawing didn't look weird enough, so I tried even harder to make them even weirder.

Ultimately, it was a total failure and this lot didn't work at all, but I went back to my old style with renewed enthusiasm and I doubt anyone else noticed. It's good to question yourself though, make sure you're not just going through the motions.

Needless to say, I had a ball with all the Colin Clues in those boxes. Can you spot them all?

Answers below, but no prizes!

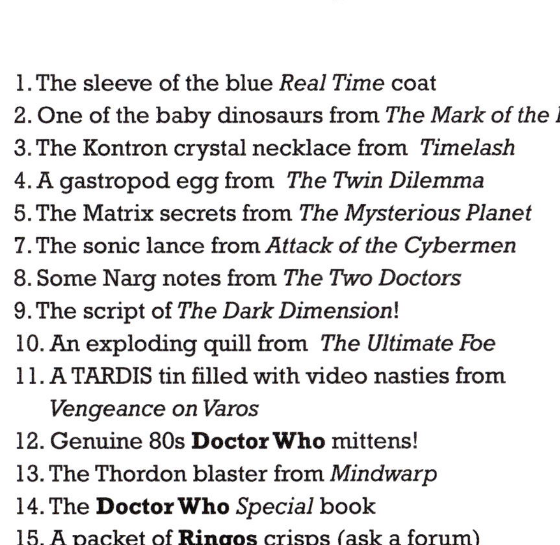

1. The sleeve of the blue *Real Time* coat
2. One of the baby dinosaurs from *The Mark of the Rani*
3. The Kontron crystal necklace from *Timelash*
4. A gastropod egg from *The Twin Dilemma*
5. The Matrix secrets from *The Mysterious Planet*
7. The sonic lance from *Attack of the Cybermen*
8. Some Narg notes from *The Two Doctors*
9. The script of *The Dark Dimension*!
10. An exploding quill from *The Ultimate Foe*
11. A TARDIS tin filled with video nasties from *Vengeance on Varos*
12. Genuine 80s **Doctor Who** mittens!
13. The Thordon blaster from *Mindwarp*
14. The **Doctor Who** *Special* book
15. A packet of **Ringos** crisps (ask a forum)
16. A Vervoid leaf from *Terror of the Vervoids*
17. An imperial plunger from *Revelation of the Daleks*
18. The Doctor's rainbow umbrella

DOCTOR WHOAH!
by baxter
Katy Manning, Louise Jameson and Janet Fielding reminisce about BBC TV Centre...
LEGEND
GENIUS
IN MY DAY, WE ONLY HAD AN AFTERNOON TO REHEARSE, A DRESSING ROOM THE SIZE OF A BROOM CUPBOARD, AND IF YOU FORGOT YOUR LINES YOU HAD TO KISS JOHN LEVENE...
YOU HAD IT EASY! WE ONLY HAD AN HOUR TO REHEARSE, WE HAD TO SHARE THE BROOM CUPBOARD WITH THE CAST OF GRANGE HILL, AND IF WE MISSED OUR MARKS, GRAHAM WILLIAMS WOULD BEAT US WITH THE ROD OF RASSILON!
THAT'S NOTHING! WE HAD TO MAKE UP OUR LINES AS WE FILMED THEM, WE HAD TO GET CHANGED INSIDE A DALEK AND IF WE MADE ANY MISTAKES AT ALL, THEY'D WRITE ADRIC BACK INTO THE SCRIPT!!!

DOCTOR WHOAH!
by baxter
Terrible confusion as Matt Smith passes on the Olympic flame...
TA VERY MUCH, MATEY! ALLONZ-Y!
EH? I THOUGHT WE ONLY DID THIS MULTI-DOCTOR STUFF ON ANNIVERSARIES!?

DOCTOR WHOAH!
by baxter
The Doctor is taking no chances with his latest hat...
RELAX DOCTOR, RIVER'S NOT HERE.
HOW CAN YOU BE SURE???
SHE PUT A GRENADE IN MY STOVEPIPE IN 1966!
SHERF
DERPTY

DOCTOR WHO
by baxter
Low numbers force the Weeping Angels to recruit other statues from New York City...
RIGHT, MISTER... LINCOLN – HAVE YOU HAD MUCH EXPERIENCE IN WEEPING, OR SENDING PEOPLE BACK THROUGH TIME?
WELL NO, NOT REALLY, BUT MY HAT IS EXCEPTIONALLY TALL...

DOCTOR WHOAH!
by baxter
The Doctor runs into
the late Brigadier's daughter...
HOW DID
YOU KNOW?
ERR...LUCKY
GUESS?
AMBU
-LENSE
GROWN-UP
PANTS
FIDDLE
FADDLE

Now I don't know who made the call on this one, but as far as I can see this character probably didn't need to be the Brig's daughter in order for the story to work, and she definitely didn't need to be called 'Kate'.

But she was, and that little link to the character that appeared in those books and short films from the 'Wilderness Years' with no **Doctor Who** on telly is very precious and shows what love goes into making the programme.

The gag's a bit obvious but it had to be done and it was great fun to draw. It looks like I gave Rory a bit of a hard time though. Then again doesn't everybody?

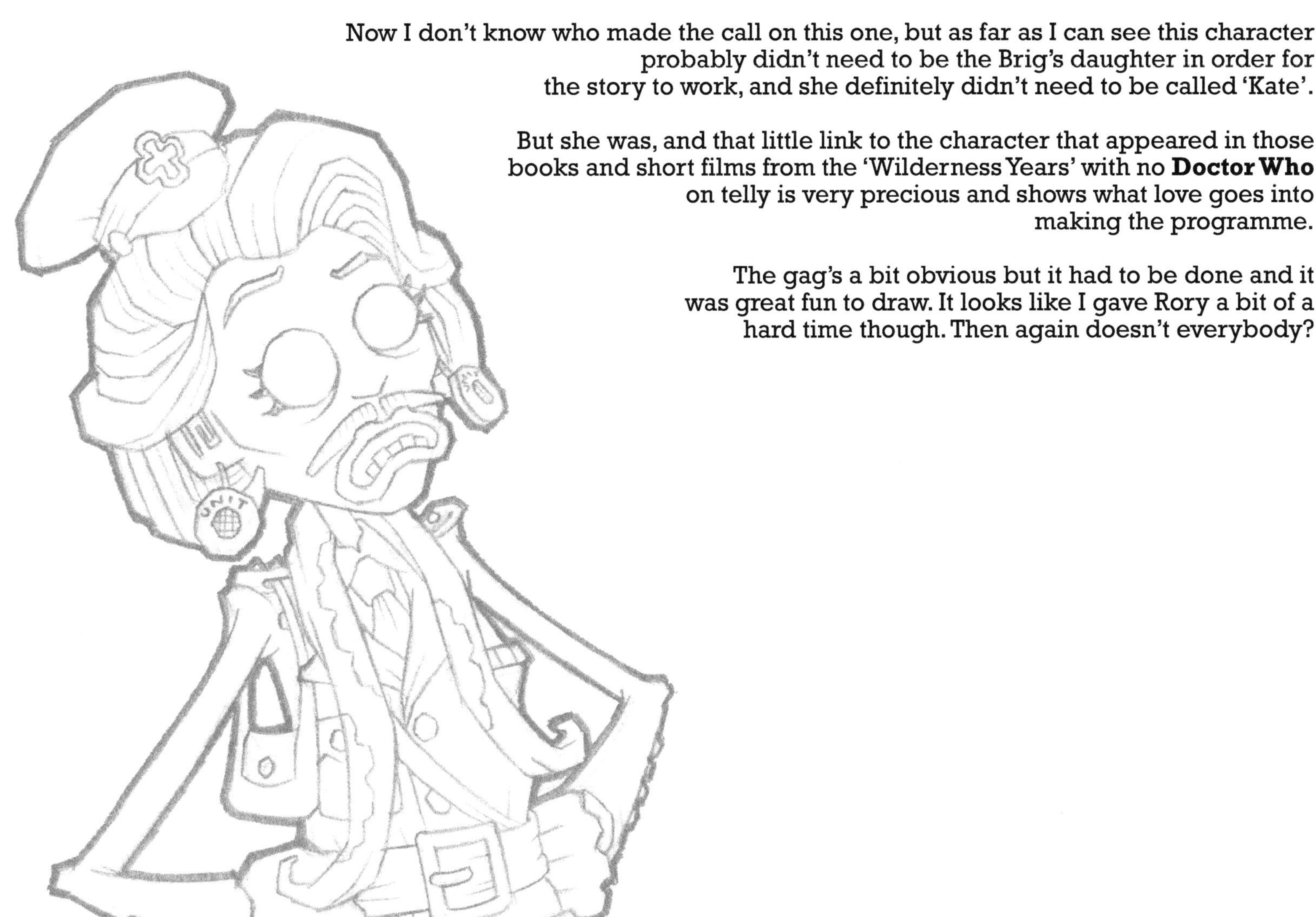

DOCTOR WHOAH!
by baxter
After the success of the Eighth Doctor's new look, all the other Big Finish Doctors get snazzy new costumes...
BEEF
BRILLIANT!
AT LAST, A DECENT COSTUME!
HEY, ALL I'VE GOT IS A NEW HAT!!!

DOCTOR WHOAH!
by baxter
ADVENT DOCTOR WHO CALENDAR
Santa's secret revealed...
SAME TIME NEXT YEAR, JEFF?
YEP. THEY STILL CAN'T WORK IT OUT, YOU KNOW!

DOCTOR
by baxter

Back with a bang!

Doctor Whoah! took a break for most of 2013 and I wasn't sure if we'd just keep going with the replacement strip (see the back of this book) but when Tom asked me to draw all Eleven Doctors having a huge party for the fiftieth anniversary issue I didn't hesitate.

To be even the tinest, most insignificant cog in the wonderful machine that is **Doctor Who** meant the world to me, and to have my own little space in such a brilliant magazine to express my feelings about the show was very special.

I've had a lot of fun over the years but I think this may well be the highlight of my career. It might even be the best of the Pertwee hair gags - what do you reckon?

DOCTOR WHOAH!
by baxter
Christmas on Karn.
ANGRY
FAT
WOMAN
BOTTOMS UP, DOCTORS!
WAIT- THAT'S NOT EGG-NOG!!!

DOCTOR WHOAH!
by baxter
Still not ginger.
DOCTOR, WHAT ARE YOU DOING?
TAKING MATTERS INTO MY OWN HANDS!
RUSTY'S RED HAIR DYE
pat

DOCTOR WHOAH!
by baxter
The Doctor fares badly on *Blind Date*.
IF I WAS YOUR NEW COMPANION . . .
WHERE WOULD YOU TAKE ME ON OUR FIRST DATE?
A HAUNTED HOUSE!
THE END OF THE WORLD!!
THE TUMMY OF A GIANT SPACE WHALE!!!
KILLA BLACK

DOCTOR WHOAH!
by baxter
Dalek creator Terry Nation claims he was inspired by the Georgian State ballet.
WELL, I CAN'T SEE IT MYSELF...
I AM 5

DOCTOR WHOAH!
by baxter
The Eighth Doctor finally gets his own catchphrase...
I'M A DOCTOR... BUT PROBABLY NOT THE ONE YOU'RE EXPECTING!
THIS HAS TO STOP.
CUT HERE↑

DOCTOR WHOAH!
by baxter
The Ice Warriors get it together.
RIGHT...
THIS TIME WE SMASH ALL THE HEATING CONTROLS FIRST!

DOCTOR WHOAH!
by baxter
PROPERTY OF VISLOR TURLOUGH
The Brigadier has lost his memories.
NOW LOOK HERE, I HAVEN'T THE FAINTEST IDEA WHO YOU ARE!
NO PROBLEM! YOU PUT YOUR FEET UP AND I'LL MAKE THE TEA!
DOCTOR WHO
WEB OF FEAR

DOCTOR WHOAH!
by baxter
KAMELION DROID INSTRUCTION MANUAL
Meanwhile, in the time vortex...
YOU TOO?! HE TREATS THIS PLACE LIKE A BLOOMIN' DUMPING GROUND!
BBC
POWER OF THE DALEKS

Well, all good things come to an end, and I thought it'd be good to get out while we were all still having fun. Plus I wouldn't have been able to do this book if it had gone on forever! I may not have beaten Tim Quinn and Dicky Howett's run but I had a good crack and I drew that question-mark pullover a lot (I love that pullover)

After all it wasn't the last **Doctor Whoah!** in the end - they're in the back of this book. But it was the last one published in **DWM** and a great one to go out on. I can't take the credit for the gag though, this one was Jonny Morris' idea.

Here are a some bits the Doctor's chucked into the void that didn't make it into the strip.

Sorry Axos!

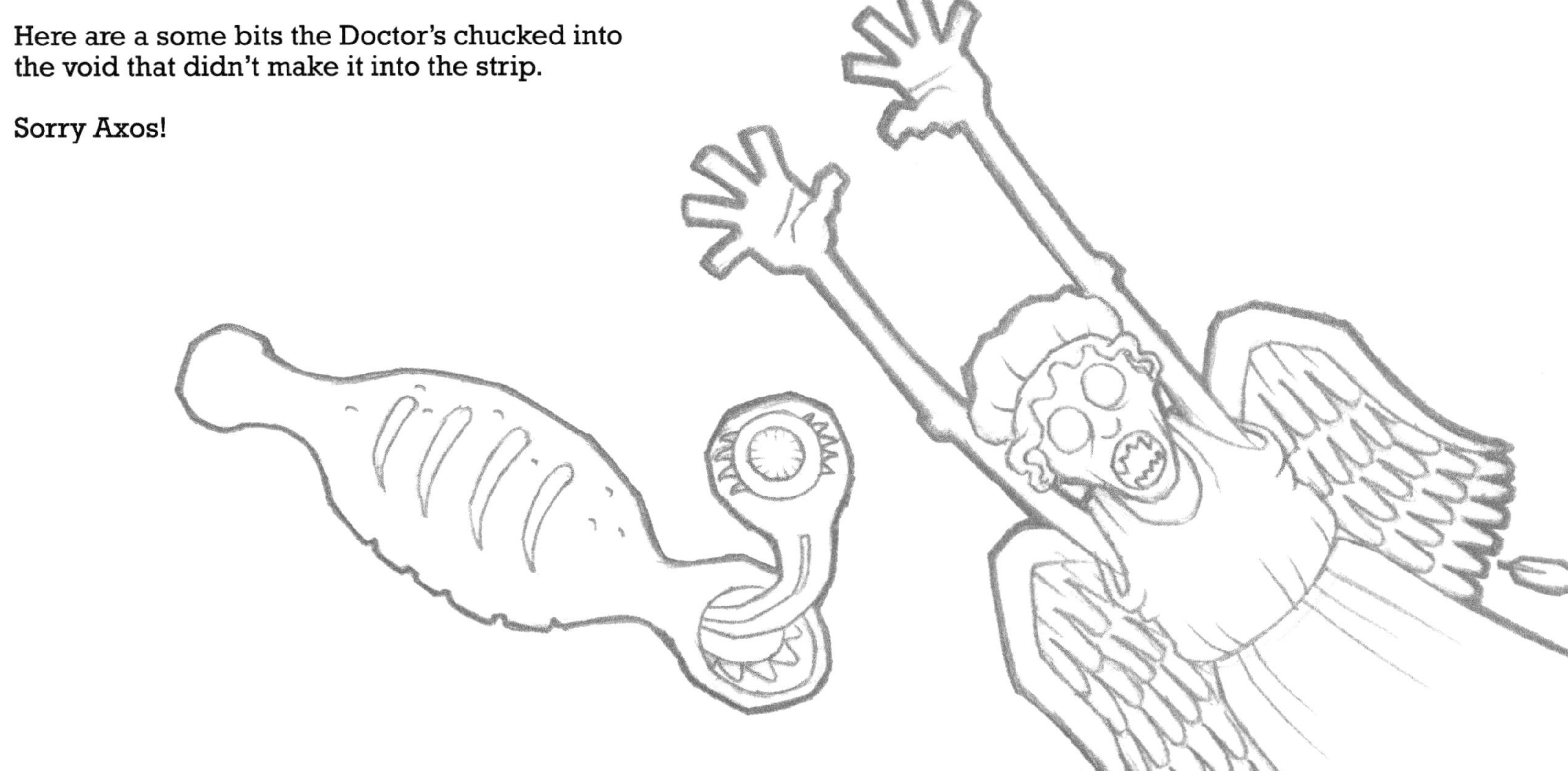

HIDDEN EXTRAS

Here's a couple of unpublished bits and bobs from the very first scribblings of ideas I had for the strip through the gradual shaping and refining, led by then-editor Clayton Hickman, until we have more or less the finished product. A couple of these practice runs ended up reworked and published years later - including Clay's favourite, 'The Ex Doctors Club', which went through a few versions.

When I first submitted my ideas I'm ashamed to say I hadn't been keeping up with **DWM** and my memories were still of those 90s issues, partly black and white and forced to plunder the history of the show for material, and the demo strips reflected this.

I was terrified of working in colour but Clay was right to insist upon it, as well as gags that focussed on the new series, which we hadn't seen much of at that time. Unfamiliar territory!

These are followed by one strip about 'Doctor Who Live' that was done for the magazine but never published for some reason, and then a few personal faves that I always wanted to draw but never got picked by the editors. I completed them specially for this collection and it was great fun. Enjoy!

DOCTOR WHAT
by baxter
2008: BBCi announce their casting choice for the Tenth Doctor - it's Danny from Withnail and I!
SOD IT, LET'S JUST CAST THE LOT OF THEM!
BBC EXECUTIVE
BOOZE!
BOOZE!
MY DEAR BRIGADIER, IF I MEDICINED YOU...

DOCTOR WHAT
by baxter
Still reeling from the shock of the 'Merlin' revelation, the Seventh Doctor travels further forward into his own personal time stream and discovers that he is destined to become George Formby.
POLICE BOX
BOX
OH, YOU SHOULD SEE WHAT I CAN SEE, WHEN I'M FREEZIN' DAVROS...
WINK
PLINK PLINK

DOCTOR WHAT
by baxter
The Cybermen face their deadliest enemy...MR T!!!
RUN!
ARGH!
RUUUUUUN!
ARGH!!! SO MUCH GOLD!!!
I PITY THE FOOL THAT DON'T HAVE NO EMOTIONS

DOCTOR WHAT
by baxter
As news of Christopher Eccleston's casting hits, Paul McGann is comforted by George Lazenby, and Colin Baker is releived of the weighty title of 'fewest episodes'. Amid the chaos, Richard E. Grant steals a word or two with Richard Hurndall and Peter Cushing.
WHIMPER... ERIC ROBERTS...
CRACKING!
WHAT ARE WE THEN? AM I THE NINTH DOCTOR OR WHAT?
DON'T LOOK AT ME MATE. WE BOTH PLAYED THE FIRST DOCTOR. YOU'RE A CARTOON.
I WAS THE ONLY ONE WITH A MOUSTACHE, YOU KNOW

DOCTOR WHAT by baxter

Billie Piper totally freaks out at the sight of David Tennant's mole.

DOCTOR WHAT
by baxter
1975: Bad communication between Terry Nation and the BBC Design department means that Davros' original costume is never used.
YOU SAID "HALF MAN, HALF DALEK"!

DOCTOR WHAT
by baxter
The Ninth Doctor and Rose visit Skrodulon Five, one of the few planets in the universe which does not have a north.
EH UP, OUR KID!
YOU WOT GUV? OOZ KID?
WOSSIE ON ABAHT?

DOCTOR WHAT
by baxter
2004: As the news of Christopher Eccleston's casting hits, Paul McGann is comforted by George Lazenby, and Colin Baker is releived of the weighty title of 'fewest episodes'. Amid the chaos, Richard E. Grant steals a word or two with Richard Hurndall and Peter Cushing.
WHAT ARE WE THEN? AM I THE NINTH DOCTOR OR WHAT?
DON'T LOOK AT ME MATE. WE BOTH PLAYED THE FIRST DOCTOR. YOU'RE A CARTOON.
I WAS THE ONLY ONE WITH A MOUSTACHE, YOU KNOW

DOCTOR WHAT
by baxter
The burping wheelie bin from *Rose* makes a bad impression at curry night.
I'M SORRY ABOUT HIM. IT MUST BE ALL THAT FANTA HE'S HAD
BRAARP
NO HOT ASH

DOCTOR WHOAH!
by baxter
Highlights from Doctor Who Live, with some of the last series' most exciting monsters.
LOOK! IT'S PRISONER ZERO!
YIKES! AN EKNODINE!
WOW! THE TOTALLY INVISIBLE CREATURE FROM "VINCENT AND THE DOCTOR"!

DOCTOR WHOAH!
by baxter
By the time of *Logopolis*, Tom Baker's Doctor had become so morose he had actually turned into a floating ball of burgundy wool.
DOCTOR, LOGOPOLIS IS DYING! THE CAUSAL NEXUS
OH BOO HOO! EVERYONE'S DYING WHEN YOU THINK ABOUT IT...

DOCTOR WHOAH!
by baxter
The Doctor enlists the help of an old friend to help defeat the Cyberking.
BIFF
SO YOU STILL SEE SARAH THEN, DOCTOR? DOES SHE EVER ASK ABOUT ME?
OH YEAH, ALL THE TIME! I'LL GIVE YOU HER NUMBER WHEN WE'RE DONE WITH THIS!

DOCTOR WHOA
by baxter
A rare on-set photo of
the original TARDIS crew,
including unsung hero
Tim *'The Time Rotor'* Taylor.

REGENERATION

Doctor Whoah! survived several re-designs at **DWM**, a time when content gets shaken up and often some long-standing features are retired.

On occasion, the team and I would try and come up with a different cartoon with a different look to replace **Doctor Whoah!**, and here are some of those attempts, all of which I still find very funny and would have enjoyed working on for however long they'd lasted.

This gave me a chance, as **DWM** always has, to stretch my skills (such as they are) and experiment with new styles. One of them was even worked up as a gag for the main strip, as you've seen.

Eventually, we came up with a new strip for the 50th anniversary year called **Moments In Time**, reflecting on each of the Doctors on turn. These eleven strips are presented here for your pleasure.

THE UNIVERSAL DATABANK
FACTOID #239605
BEFORE HE BECAME EDITOR OF SATELLITE FIVE,"THE EDITOR" WAS EDITOR OF "SMASH HITS" MAGAZINE FOR TWENTY YEARS. HE IS CREDITED WITH MANY INNOVATIONS, INCLUDING "FAMOUS BOTTOMS" AND THE FREE COMB WITH ISSUE #3765894574.

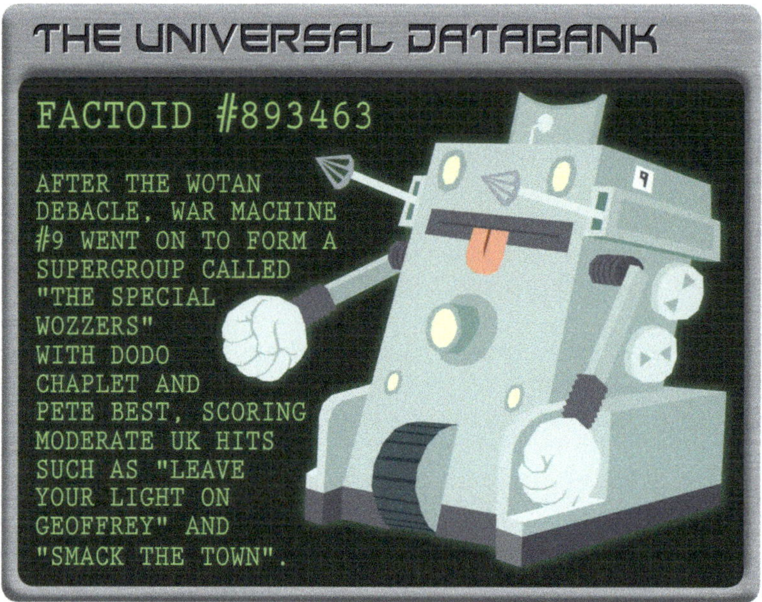
THE UNIVERSAL DATABANK
FACTOID #893463
AFTER THE WOTAN DEBACLE, WAR MACHINE #9 WENT ON TO FORM A SUPERGROUP CALLED "THE SPECIAL WOZZERS" WITH DODO CHAPLET AND PETE BEST, SCORING MODERATE UK HITS SUCH AS "LEAVE YOUR LIGHT ON GEOFFREY" AND "SMACK THE TOWN".
9

THE MIND PROBE by jamie lenman

ORIGINAL ART BY GERRY HAYLOCK

MOMENTS IN TIME
SUSAN! WHAT ARE YOU DOING IN THIS JUNKYARD?
AND WHY ARE YOU STUCK IN THAT OLD SENTRY BOX?
POLICE BOX
POLICE BOX
WELL IT'S AN EASY MISTAKE. STUPID THING WAS AN OIL DRUM LAST WEEK...
BY JAMIE LENMAN

MOMENTS IN TIME
LOOK AT THE SIZE OF THAT THING, DOCTOR!
YES JAMIE, THAT IS A BIG ONE...
BY JAMIE LENMAN

MOMENTS IN TIME
AH, DOCTOR! LET ME INTRODUCE YOU TO OUR NEW CORPORAL. "RESTAM EHT!"
EHT
ARE YOU SERIOUS?
BY JAMIE LENMAN

MOMENTS IN TIME
BUT DOCTOR, YOU SAID NO KILLING!
NO, I SAID NO JANIS THORNS. BAZOOKA IS TOTALLY FINE.
BY JAMIE LENMAN

MOMENTS IN TIME
HAPPY BIRTHDAY, DOCTOR!
SSSSSSSSSSS
THANKS, TURLOUGH!
IT'S NOT YOUR BIRTHDAY...
BY JAMIE LENMAN

MOMENTS IN TIME
HE HAS ESCAPED INTO THE PATCHWORK JUNGLE!
WE WILL NEVER FIND HIM NOW...
BY JAMIE LENMAN

MOMENTS IN TIME
SALE
THAT ONE!
BY

MOMENTS IN TIME
NO, DEFINITELY GO FOR THE 'WILD BILL HICOCK' LOOK...
BY JAMIE LENMAN

MOMENTS IN TIME
MATE, WITH ALL THE TIMEY-WIMEY NONSENSE HEADING MY WAY, I WOULDN'T RULE IT OUT.
ARE YOU MY MUMMY?
BY JAMIE LENMAN

MOMENTS IN TIME
THAT...IS UNFORTUNATE.
BY JAMIE LENMAN

MOMENTS IN TIME
VICTORY AT LAST!!!
FIRE EXIT
BY JAMIE LENMAN

PLEASE BOX
PLEASE BOX
TEA 50P

ALSO AVAILABLE FROM **MIWK PUBLISHING**

HOODED MAN

Volumes One and Two

'In the days of the Lion spawned of the Devil's Brood, the Hooded Man shall come to the forest. There he will meet Herne the Hunter, Lord of the Trees, and be his son and do his bidding. The Powers of Light and Darkness shall be strong within him. And the guilty shall tremble.'

With its distinctive mixture of history and mythology, Robin of Sherwood was an innovative treatment of the Robin Hood legend. Broadcast on ITV between 1984 and 1986, the series has been a major influence on later versions of the Robin Hood story.

Now for the first time, a guide to the series in two volumes, from its beginnings in fifteenth century ballads of Robin Hood to its modern tale of a band of guerrillas striking from their forest hideout.

Hooded Man Volumes One and Two take a fresh look at each episode starring Michael Praed and Jason Connery. It explores the production of every series and the legends, literature and history that influenced them. You'll find new trivia, goofs, quotes and translations, a comprehensive atlas of filming locations and the full story of the creation of the series. Also included is a comprehensive guide to the spin-off material, including the novelisations and gamebooks, the *Touchstones of Rhiannon* computer game, and a complete analysis of all 126 issues of the comic strip.

Hooded Man is an essential guide for every true fan of the series, detailing everything you might have missed along the way... *because nothing is ever forgotten.*

Volume One includes a foreword by the producer Esta Charkham, and Volume Two a foreword by Jason Connery.

ISBN 978-1-908630-05-6 **ISBN** 978-1-908630-62-9

www.miwk.com/

www.facebook.com/MiwkPublishingLtd

www.twitter.com/#!/MiwkPublishing